W9-AHG-936

SEEDS, BULBS, AND SPROUTS

DEVI PURI

New York

J 581.4
Puri

Published in 2016 by The Rosen Publishing Group, Inc.
29 East 21st Street, New York, NY 10010

Copyright © 2016 by The Rosen Publishing Group, Inc.

All rights reserved. No part of this book may be reproduced in any form without permission in writing from the publisher, except by a reviewer.

First Edition

Editor: Sarah Machajewski
Book Design: Michael J. Flynn

Photo Credits: Cover (bulbs and tools on table) Africa Studio/Shutterstock.com; cover (seeds) Mona Makela/Shutterstock.com; cover (potted seedlings) Elena Elisseeva/Shutterstock.com; back cover, pp. 3–4, 6, 8–11, 13–16, 18–20, 23–24 (soil) Andrey_Kuzmin/Shutterstock.com; p. 5 gorillaimages/Shutterstock.com; p. 7 Marie C Fields/Shutterstock.com; p. 9 Artography/Shutterstock.com; p. 10 Jake Wyman/The Image Bank/Getty Images; p. 11 Ilike/Shutterstock.com; p. 12 Grisha Bruev/Shutterstock.com; p. 13 mayakova/Shutterstock.com; p. 14 yasuhiro amano/Shutterstock.com; p. 15 Monkey Business Images/Shutterstock.com; p. 16 leungchopan/Shutterstock.com; p. 17 (daffodil) joingate/Shutterstock.com; p. 17 (onion) unpict/Shutterstock.com; p. 19 (tulips) Anteromite/Shutterstock.com; p. 19 (bulbs) V. J. Matthew/Shutterstock.com; p. 21 (gardens) StevanZZ/Shutterstock.com; p. 21 (potted flowers) Dirk Ott/Shutterstock.com; p. 22 Sergiy Bykhunenko/Shutterstock.com.

Library of Congress Cataloging-in-Publication Data

Puri, Devi, author.
  Seeds, bulbs, and sprouts / Devi Puri.
      pages cm. — (Garden squad!)
  Includes bibliographical references and index.
  ISBN 978-1-4994-0977-2 (pbk.)
  ISBN 978-1-4994-1000-6 (6 pack)
  ISBN 978-1-4994-1018-1 (library binding)
  1. Seeds—Juvenile literature. 2. Bulbs (Plants)—Juvenile literature. 3. Sprouts—Juvenile literature. I. Title. II. Series: Garden squad!
  QK661.P87 2016
  581.4'67—dc23
                                        2015015164

Manufactured in the United States of America

CPSIA Compliance Information: Batch #WS15PK: For Further Information contact Rosen Publishing, New York, New York at 1-800-237-9932

CONTENTS

UNDERSTANDING PLANT PARTS.... 4

ALL ABOUT SEEDS 6

PARTS OF A SEED 8

GROWING SEEDS 10

GERMINATION 12

CARING FOR SPROUTS. 14

BEAUTIFUL BULBS 16

CARING FOR BULBS 18

PLANNING YOUR GARDEN 20

GET DIGGING! 22

GLOSSARY 23

INDEX 24

WEBSITES 24

UNDERSTANDING PLANT PARTS

If there's anyone who's familiar with how plants live and grow, it's gardeners. Gardeners use simple science to create beautiful **landscapes**. They know that sunlight, water, and air—as well as hard work—can turn tiny seeds into full-grown plants.

As they grow, plants go through different life stages. Seeds are one of them. Sprouts are another. Some plants contain all their life stages in a **structure** called a bulb. Each of these plant stages is special, and gardeners must know how to handle them. Understanding the science behind seeds, bulbs, and sprouts is one of the first steps to having a great garden.

GARDEN GUIDE

Good soil is needed to grow healthy plants. Before you sow seeds or plant sprouts or bulbs, make sure your soil is healthy and full of **nutrients**.

Seeds, bulbs, and sprouts are the building blocks of gardens.

ALL ABOUT SEEDS

Gardeners have many choices when it comes to deciding what to plant. If you're a first-time gardener, you may have fun experimenting with plants in different stages of their lives. The first stage, of course, is a seed.

A seed is a tiny, hard object. Seeds come in many different shapes, colors, and sizes. Some seeds are hard, and others are soft. Some seeds can be eaten, while eating others could make you sick. It depends on what kind of plant the seed comes from. Even though all seeds are different, they share the same basic features.

These seeds may grow into colorful flowers, tasty vegetables, flavorful **herbs**, or beautiful green plants. There are no limits to what kinds of seeds you can plant.

PARTS OF A SEED

A seed contains everything a plant needs to grow. That includes a tiny plant called an **embryo**, as well as the food the embryo needs. In flowering plants, this food is called endosperm.

The embryo and endosperm are very important. A seed can't produce a plant if these parts are damaged, or hurt. However, the seed coat, or outer covering, keeps this from happening. The seed coat **protects** the tiny plant from harm. In your garden, a seed could be harmed by bad weather or an animal looking for food. A gardener who steps on a seed could crush the baby plant without a seed coat to protect it!

GARDEN GUIDE

Seeds germinate, or sprout, when they have enough sunlight, water, and air. When it germinates, the seed coat opens and the tiny plant begins growing toward the light.

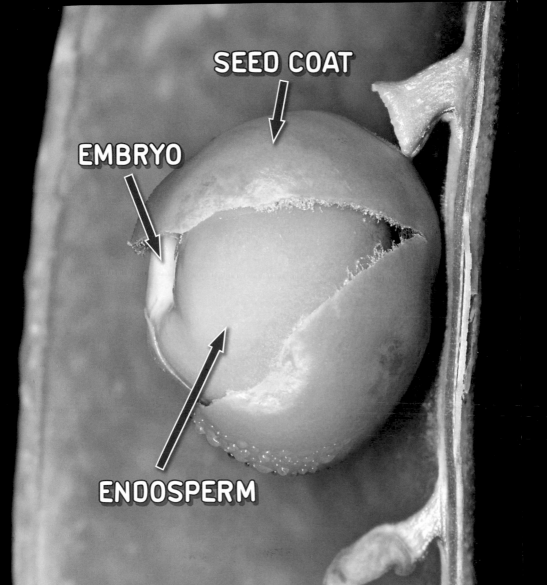

SEED COAT

EMBRYO

ENDOSPERM

A seed coat also keeps the inside of a seed from drying out.

GROWING SEEDS

Seeds come from flowers and fruits. The flowers in your garden may drop seeds, which can be used to grow more plants. You can buy seed packets at the store or from the Internet. You can also ask a fellow gardener to do a seed swap.

GARDEN GUIDE

Different seeds may need different amounts of water, sunlight, and air to germinate. Read the directions on the back of a seed packet before you start planting.

Sow seeds evenly so the plants have room to grow. Press your finger into the soil and place the seed in the hole. Cover the seed with a thin **layer** of soil, and then water it.

Once you have seeds, you can plant them directly in the ground or in pots. Many gardeners use seed-starting trays. They're made of small squares that each hold a seed. Gardeners like using trays because they can control the warmth and light the seeds get. It also allows gardeners to start plants before the weather is warm enough to plant outside.

GERMINATION

Once a seed germinates, the tiny plant grows up toward the surface of your garden. Its roots grow down into the soil. You should see tiny plants poking through the soil a few days or weeks after you plant seeds. These tiny plants are called sprouts.

A sprout looks like the plant that will grow in your garden, but smaller. Sprouts have a stem and tiny leaves, called true leaves. The leaves begin the process of photosynthesis. This is when the leaves take in sunlight and carbon dioxide, which is a gas in the air. Plants combine them with water and nutrients from the soil to make food for the plant.

TRUE LEAVES

STEM

Seeing sprouts for the first time is an exciting gardening moment. It's proof that all your hard work is paying off!

CARING FOR SPROUTS

Sprouts are very **delicate**, so you must handle them with care. The roots, stems, and leaves aren't strong enough yet to hold up against something harmful. What harms sprouts? People or animals stepping on sprouts can kill them. Too much water can drown the roots. Too much cold can hurt them, too.

Once your garden has sprouted, you may notice some areas have more sprouts than others. Empty areas mean the seeds you planted there didn't germinate. That's okay—carefully dig up some sprouts and **transplant** them to the empty areas. That way, each sprout has enough room to grow.

Some plant sprouts can be tasty salad or sandwich toppings. They're picked before the plant has a chance to grow any further. Bean sprouts are a popular choice.

GARDEN GUIDE

Some gardeners skip seeds and go straight to sprouts. You can buy sprouted plants, or seedlings, from a garden store. Plant them directly in the soil, but be careful to not harm the roots or tiny plant parts.

BEAUTIFUL BULBS

Most plants have a life cycle that begins with a seed, which grows into a sprout, and then into an adult plant. These stages are easy to see. Bulbs are different. Bulbs are plants whose whole life cycle is stored in a structure that grows underground.

True bulbs have five parts. Roots grow from the bottom. They take in water and nutrients. Fleshy scales store food for the bulb. A covering called a tunic protects the scales. Bulblets grow off the main structure to make more bulbs. Finally, bulbs have a shoot. It holds the part of the plant we see aboveground.

BULBLET

Tulips, daffodils, and hyacinths are popular bulbs. Alliums are another common type of bulb. This plant group includes onions, garlic, and shallots.

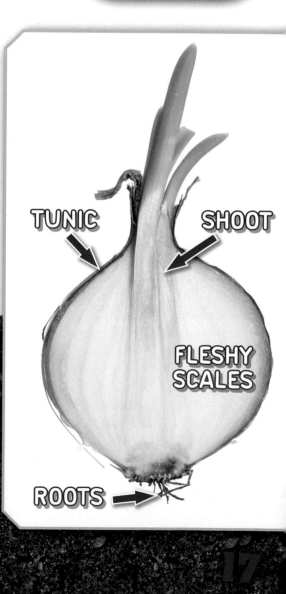

TUNIC

SHOOT

FLESHY SCALES

ROOTS

CARING FOR BULBS

The way you plant bulbs is different from how you normally garden. For starters, bulbs are planted in the fall. They can be planted up until the ground freezes. However, it's still important to make sure your soil is healthy and full of nutrients.

Plant bulbs between six and eight inches (15 cm and 20 cm) deep in the ground. Cover them with soil—then wait. You won't see your plants until spring. During this time, the bulbs become **dormant**. When the soil warms, the bulbs come to life. The shoots grow aboveground, sending leaves and a flower with them.

GARDEN GUIDE

Bulbs are planted in fall because the cool soil makes them produce roots. The roots stop growing when the soil freezes, but they don't die.

These tulip plants grow through snow-covered soil. Tulips are a sure sign that spring is on its way!

PLANNING YOUR GARDEN

Now that you know the basics of seeds, bulbs, and sprouts, how can you choose what to do with them? Start by thinking about what kind of garden you'd like to grow. If you're set on growing plants from seeds, vegetable gardening can be a good place to start. Many beginning gardeners have luck with beans, carrots, and peas.

Some gardeners prefer to begin with sprouts, or seedlings. It can be easier and faster than waiting for seeds to germinate. Bulbs are a good choice for gardeners who want to save money because they only need to be planted once—they come back every year.

The way your garden looks is completely up to you. Try planting seeds in pots and seedlings directly in the ground. Plant bulbs where you'd like to see the same plants year after year.

GET DIGGING!

Understanding plant parts is important to becoming a good gardener. If you don't know how a seed germinates, you may not give it all the water and light it needs. Without understanding how bulbs wake up after a winter of being dormant, you may plant them in an area where soil doesn't get warm enough. Handling sprouts too roughly won't allow them to grow.

However, it only takes a little bit of effort to become familiar with each of these special plant parts. Once you do, your garden will be bigger and better than you could've ever imagined!

GLOSSARY

delicate: Easily broken or harmed.

dormant: Alive but not actively growing.

embryo: The part of a seed that grows into a plant.

herb: A plant with leaves, seeds, or flowers that are used to flavor food or make medicine.

landscape: The visible features of an area of land.

layer: One thickness lying over or under another.

nutrient: Something a living thing needs to grow and stay alive.

protect: To keep safe.

structure: An object made of several parts.

transplant: To replant in another place.

INDEX

A
adult plant, 4, 16
air, 4, 8, 10, 12

B
bulblets, 16
bulbs, 4, 5, 16, 17, 18, 20, 22

E
embryo, 8, 9
endosperm, 8, 9

F
fleshy scales, 16, 17
flowers, 6, 8, 10, 18
fruits, 10

G
germinate, 8, 10, 12, 14, 20, 22

L
leaves, 12, 14, 18

N
nutrients, 4, 12, 16, 18

P
photosynthesis, 12

R
roots, 12, 14, 15, 16, 17, 18

S
seed coat, 8, 9
seedlings, 15, 20
seeds, 4, 5, 6, 8, 9, 10, 11, 12, 14, 15, 16, 20, 22
shoot, 16, 17, 18
soil, 4, 11, 12, 15, 18, 19, 22
sprouts, 4, 5, 12, 13, 14, 15, 16, 20, 22
stem, 12, 13, 14
sunlight, 4, 8, 10, 12

T
true leaves, 12, 13
tunic, 16, 17

W
water, 4, 8, 10, 11, 12, 14, 16, 22

WEBSITES

Due to the changing nature of Internet links, PowerKids Press has developed an online list of websites related to the subject of this book. This site is updated regularly. Please use this link to access the list: www.powerkidslinks.com/grdn/bulb